PEZ

Earth Time
Water and Sky

Haibun
& Haiku

Jo Pacsoo

Earth Time, Water and Sky

PALORES PUBLICATIONS' 21st CENTURY WRITERS

Jo Pacsoo
Earth Time, Water and Sky

Copyright © Jo Pascoo 2005

October 2005

ISBN 0-9547985-9-7

Designed and printed by:

ImageSet,
63 Tehidy Road,
Camborne,
Cornwall. TR14 8LJ
01209 712864

Published by:

Palores Publications,
11a Penryn Street, Redruth,
Cornwall TR15 2SP

Typeset in Garamond 10/11pt

Earth Time, Water and Sky
HAIKU & HAIBUN

Ultimately haiku eludes definition.
Cor van den Heuvel *The Haiku Anthology*

I am not trying to define haiku or haibun but to offer a few thoughts on my personal approach for those who are unfamiliar with these forms.

English haiku are a recent adaptation of a form which has a long history in Japan. Haiku are brief poems, simple understatements of small, transient details of life. The sparseness and lack of subjective or intellectual interpretation allow the reader to participate in the rawness of experience. Haiku are poems which do not fit into any traditional concepts of poetry. They are expressed in concrete rather than abstract language, with no overt metaphor, personification or symbolism. (Though the haiku itself can be a metaphor.) Haiku are poems of subtlety and suggestion rather than elaboration or explication. The poet is not intrusive and the reading is open to the intuition of the reader to complete the experience.

In haibun the haiku are embedded in a wider context, enabling a journey through the piece in connection, or often in parallel with, the haiku. Like haiku, the prose in haibun is also succinct and understated, sometimes so brief as to be ungrammatical, with no explicit judgements, emotions or conclusions.

Both haiku and haibun invite the reader to enter into their open-endedness, to be present to the immediacy of life. The aim is not to capture life but to appreciate its transience. The briefness aims to convey more than is expressed. These pieces come from events in my own life but I hope you will find some resonance with the wider field of human (and non-human) life and experience.

Thanks to all those who have guided my Haiku journey.

These pieces have previously been Published in:

Blithe Spirit, Presence, Time Haiku, Poetry Cornwall, Frogpond (USA), Contemporary Haibun Anthology (USA)

Earth Time, Water and Sky

the quiet of fading day
a foxcub
in the open doorway

contemplating
death - the yellowness
of kingcups

in the still night
uneasy together
hoot of a train

in the kitchen
after viewing Mars
the smell of apples

eighteen years since
my mother died - still
using her toothpicks

Earth Time

dawn coolness
sound of a thrush
breaking snails

at the end of a dark lane
face to face with
a barn owl

the longest night
time to make
a will

behind
a lumbering badger
the field in moonlight

the shortest day
shadows ripple the bank
a white egret

Time Walk

We set out along the beach. A horse thuds by at full gallop, rider plodding after. Caves and mine adits drip with water, walls streaked red ochre, turquoise with tin and copper ores, the deserted cliffs once busy with pumping engines, crushing machines, shafts, railways, furnaces. At the end of the cliffs we turn inland, struggle up the sliding dunes.

> uphill
> from the sea
> into silence

The remains of a stone chapel lie beneath our feet. For centuries covered and revealed by shifting sand, it was buried in 1980 beneath a granite slab, to protect it from final destruction by vandals. It is said that St Piran, who floated from Ireland on a millstone, here established a monastic settlement in the 6th century. Surrounded by empty sandhills, I imagine the scene. A bell summons the monks to prayer; their chants rise above a clatter of pots from the kitchen. A novice hoes the vegetable garden, stoops to collect water from the pool.

The pool has dried up since our last visit. Piezometers stick out of the sand measuring levels of ground water. Over the fence red signs warn of military DANGER

We continue our way inland to an old granite cross beside the remnants of a Norman Church. Only the tops of the walls are above the sand. Crouching in the ruins we eat the last mince pie. Wind blows through the three-eyed cross, all traces of carving long worn away. We look back over the empty dunes to the chalets of a holiday camp. Back towards the coast. Golfers pause as we cross the course.

> wind-surfers skim
> the sea's edge
> the taste of tea

Earth Time, Water and Sky

The End of the Line

>   the family tree
>   small child searches
>   for her place

Throughout my childhood a huge picture of a tree hung above the stairs. In circles up the trunk were all the first sons, starting in the twelfth century, ending with my brother. The side branches bore subsequent sons and all the daughters. I was not there at all. Above the circles were painted: medals won in war, mitres for bishops, crossed swords for those who died in battle. The women's names were unmarked unless, like my father's sister, they died in childhood. Then they had a wreath of flowers.

>   my father's mother
>   carries her infant daughter
>   deep into the lake

On a trip to Switzerland we brought home old portraits. Too big for an English semi, they stayed in the loft for many years until we were preparing to move.

>   oil paint crackles
>   in the flames - my mother burns
>   my father's ancestors

The family tree escaped this bonfire and moved to our new house. For many years I counted my descent from this collection of bishops, mercenary soldiers, Vatican Guards and Karl, the fifteenth century revolutionary noted in Swiss history books.

It is only now that I do the sums. Two parents, four grandparents, eight great grandparents... In the thirty or so generations since the eleven hundreds my ancestors number around 1073741824 - including 536870912 women. I'm glad that the genes of those men of war and orthodox religion are well diluted before reaching my being.

Clearing out the past I take the family china to Oxfam. My brother telephones: *I've reframed the family tree, put on you and your family. You always wanted to be on it when we were children.*

>   my son
>   tenderly strokes the head
>   of his sleeping child

Waiting

My cousin writes from Australia. He tells me of his wife who is in a care home. She does not recognise him, doesn't talk. As I read I am a teenager again at a school harvest festival.

The headmistress asks for volunteers to take the offerings from our thanksgiving to the hospital. It is some time since I have seen my father and I offer to go, ask if I can take him something.

I put the fruit and flowers beside the bed, look at the shrunken body. There is no recognition in the eyes, no words on the lips.

> the night garden
> small child and her father watch
> for shooting stars

A few beds away a man is shrieking. Opposite is a blind man with no legs. He used to talk to my father but now they both wait in silence.

A nurse asks if I will give my father his supper. I hold a cup with a spout to his mouth, spoon in the food.

> a long wait
> at the bus stop
> the rain tastes of salt

In The Dark

> on midnight
> skyline
> a darker shape

Chun Quoit, neolithic dolmen: a massive boulder caps four uprights forming a small chamber.

> torchlight
> among the stones
> a frog hops

Head first we worm our way in. I am to sleep here and my companion will watch for rapid eye movements and wake me to record my dreams. It's a research programme to see if there is any correlation between the dreams of different dreamers at certain ancient sites. There is just room to lie down; I snuggle into my sleeping bag. My friend crouches beside me with red torch and tape recorder. The radioactive count is more than double that outside. 9 tons of rock balance above my head. Others have seen coloured lights; darkness enfolds me. In the silence 5,000 years of human story. Images from the past dance through my mind. Several times I'm just drifting off to sleep when I'm wakened by the red torch on my eyes. The summer night is short.

> darkness
> cracks into
> shapes of stones

I wake to find my watcher asleep. I rouse him and he records my dreams. We wriggle out into the morning.

> in the misty
> moorland space
> which path?

Middle Street

The town is deserted in the early afternoon. With the turn of the tide a warm wind tempers the tropical heat. I turn into the Promenade gardens.

> lush blooms
> invite -
> the droning bee

A place for solitude in spite of the many warnings. An Englishwoman was murdered here by a madman. She stops off for the day from a ship and is stabbed in these gardens while her doctor husband looks round the Public Hospital. He is called to an emergency and finds the dead body of his dear wife - everyone adds the endearment. They tell this as though it was recent but it happened ten years ago.

> nectar drips
> iguana
> gulps air

Middle Street. Empty apart from one old man. As he comes near he starts to speak, words blurred by thick accent.

> pink tongue
> flickers among
> yellow teeth

Accusations about slavery! Shiny black nose on worn grey face, bloodshot eyes under sagging lids, quivering tongue. He follows me for a few yards and then turns away.

> in the silence
> soft breeze
> scent of flowers

It is 1966. There are still those who remember accounts by parents or grandparents of their lives as slaves. The sins of my ancestors - slavery, opium wars, colonial exploitation... In England I have become a foreigner through marriage; here my presence is oppression.

> home
> hospital gates
> clang shut

Hallelujah

> straw huts on white sand
> beneath palm trees old men
> sit and talk

My tentative smile fades before the blank stare of the young woman. There is not much conversation between us as we unpack the boxes of books. Six of us have come by jeep, over the rough savannah, to this woman's village We are part of a UN project: *To increase the standard of living of Amerindians and integrate them into the mainstream of Guyanese society while encouraging the revival of their culture as a contribution to the sum total of Guyanese culture.* The atmosphere of the village is one of apathy. Indigenous culture has been destroyed. The people suffer from malnutrition and worms. The staple diet is cassava bread. This was once supported by hunting but pre-Independence troubles have resulted in the confiscation of all guns. The skills of bow and arrow have been lost.

> women weave colours
> into palm-string hammocks
> small girl brings water

Our group includes a doctor, an engineer, a nutritionist, an agronomist. My role is to organise a library and to look into the Amerindian encounter with missionaries. In the early 1800s Amerindian culture was vibrant. They absorbed the Christian message into tribal mythology:

The first prophet is Bichiwung of the Macusi tribe. He goes to England to learn Christianity. He suspects the priest of deceiving him and follows the dream path to meet God himself. God tells him that the white man's religion is out of date. He gives Bichiwung a new religion for the Amerindian people, teaches him songs, gives him a bottle of medicine and writings on paper. This new religion, **Hallelujah,** *will bring the people power, wealth, strength and light, akwa, tribal regeneration. Bichiwung teaches Hallelujah to his tribe but others are jealous of his power and kill him. Twice Bichiwung's wife restores him to life with the medicine God had given him. The third time his body is cut up and scattered in the foest. His wife can not find all the pieces and he remains dead. God takes Hallelujah away from the Macusi and gives it to the Akawaio. Uriah is their prophet. God calls him Abel. Christ is a rival prophet in another village but Christ dies leaving only Abel. Abel goes to heaven in his dreams and meets monkey, jaguar, wind, ocean, nature spirits, Noah's Ark and the Angel Gabriel. He brings back a gift:* **the spirit of the heart of the people.**

Earth Time, Water and Sky

The 19th century missionaries objected to sharing their stories with Amerindian mythology. They condemned the Hallelujah prophets as the work of the devil and the way to hell. They denied *the spirit of the heart of the people*. In 1840, Awacaipa, of the Aracuna tribe, told of a vision of wealth and freedom for his people. All who killed each other would be reborn at full moon with white skin. They would drive out the invaders and claim their wealth and power. Four hundred were killed.

> straw net pulled tight
> on grated cassava root
> poison drips out

The village woman and I unpack 300 books and 300 magazines. We arrange them in cupboards made on the nearby British army base. The books have been donated. I pick up *Apple Recipes for Every Month; A Child's Garden of Verses; Pride and Prejudice...*

The others meet with the village council - men only. I wander down the long, hot path to the river. Too wide to bridge, the far bank a wall of scrub. Skin colours in brown-stained water. The wetness is cool.

Authenticity

I hold a black and white photograph; a robed figure with prominent ribs and a
serene face sits cross-legged in meditation. In many visits to the British Museum I
have never found this figure which my mother had asked them to photograph. On
the back faded words in my mother's hand: *It has power beyond the material
world for those to whom it communicates.*

****

1967. Returning from Guyana with my family flames engulf an engine; a hurricane
is blowing up. We land in Trinidad by paraffin flares in a power cut and spend
three days at the Trinidad Hilton at airline expense, while a new engine is flown in.

> cooler in the hills
> we watch a farmer
> slice cocoa pods

My mother comes to meet us at Heathrow but officials only tell her that the 'plane
has not arrived, come back tomorrow. For three days my mother returns to the
airport, the *'plane has not arrived, come tomorrow.* In London she wanders into
the British Museum. On an upper floor, behind a curtain, she sits in front of a
statue of a meditating figure. Peace flows into her. She knows that all is well.

****

With my son I take the photo to the Museum. We follow an attendant into the
basement. There, in a small room among objects piled in heaps, it stands on the
floor: about 3 feet high, a warm reddish-brown wood with traces of paint. The
whole figure radiates repose; the face is particularly tranquil - this face of
burnished wood that touched my mother, thirty years ago.

The curator is not impressed with our story. She tells us that it is an image of a
Japanese Arhat.* It is not authentic, the head is newer than the rest of it. My
mother saw it in an exhibition of fakes.

> a trace of my mother
> in my son's smile
> autumn rain

* Enlightened one

Earth Time, Water and Sky

it hangs between us
in the cold kitchen
your unspoken no

at the gate
smell of a hot road
and nettles

ash tree hangs
over a dark pool
footsteps on the bridge

museum statues
the same faces
in the Metro

windless night
woodsmoke spreads
from a quiet fire

behind the clouds
a full moon
murmur of toads

Earth Time, Water and Sky

Under the Viaduct

The A30 crosses the valley on a bridge. Beneath it, surrounded by minewaste, is an open space. Children play there on bicycles. Stolen cars are burned. An old bus appears, painted with peace slogans. We chat with a man chopping wood. In a few weeks there are two more vans, a lorry and lots of dogs. A neighbour stops me:

'Have you seen the travellers down the valley? They're a surly lot, quite rude.'
'It depends how you approach them. We always find them pleasant enough.'
'I haven't seen them myself, just heard reports. Anyway, they shouldn't be allowed. Why should they live there without paying taxes? And they're probably tapped into the water and electric down there.'
'Are they? That's enterprising!'

A few weeks later the area is crammed with vans, cars, lorries, buses. Dogs are everywhere. We feel less comfortable, stop walking through the encampment.

The rumours start: *A goat was torn to pieces by the travellers' dogs. Someone was bitten. Piles of human excrement in people's gardens. Things go missing.*

Someone breaks into our shed. We lose two demi-johns of home made wine. The MP writes in the local paper; she has had more letters of complaint about the travellers than about anything else. We write a letter of support: *waste ground...not doing any harm...life style...freedom...*

Loud shouts wake us in the night. The thump of music. We find a man in the shed. Vacant-eyed, he shambles away down the footpath.

Quiet afternoon. Picking raspberries in the sunshine. Sudden zoom of helicopters swooping low, circling. They are evicting the travellers.

The new neighbours are having a party. I'm not a party-goer but feel it would be unfriendly not to go. Until I learn it's to celebrate the expulsion of the travellers.

puddles and bare earth
traffic roars above
a broken doll

Earth Time, Water and Sky

Heavy machinery moves in bringing boulders to line the roadway. To make sure it's uninhabitable the space is filled with piles of minewaste from the nearby spoilheaps. Spring - the bare red mounds blossom with primroses, violets. The flowers die in the toxic earth. Boys make cycle runs over the humps.

> over the wasteland
> wing feathers ruffled by wind
> a kestrel hovers.

---

beneath the tree
with the buzzards' nest
pine scent in sunshine

> even in Rome
> among the traffic noise
> cockcrow at dawn

> the year's end
> seals and surfers bob in the sea
> smell of cabbage fields

out of the darkness
the mating cries
of foxes

Blue Wallpaper

Spirits as heavy as the day, I take my troubles to the wind and space of the moor, trudge up the stony track sending out a confused prayer to I know not what. The view extends as I climb higher. Suddenly a single shaft of sunlight breaks through the clouds and shines on a house below. The building disappears and reappears as the sun is clouded and shines out again. I know that I must go there, that there is something there for me. I resist this idea but eventually turn my steps towards the place. I approach the house, a ruin. A man with a gun comes from the opposite side.

'Nice day for a walk.'
'Yes,' I respond, 'I like to walk on the moors'.
'It's a grand place'. He waves his gun to indicate the sweep of the hillside.
'What do you shoot?'
'Oh, rabbits, grouse, hares, anything that moves,' he laughs.
'Do you eat them?'
'Sometimes, but I just enjoy killing them, to make dead something that was alive. There's a great sense of power.' He shoulders his gun and goes off.

> stone slabs perch
> on broken rafters   grey sky
> blue wallpaper

In front of the house a spring trickles into a small stone trough. I imagine the kettle being filled here and placed on the fire beside the blue shelves.

> rusted latch
> fragments of plates   dreams
> in the crumbling walls

Round the back, a small mound, the remains of a rubbish dump. Among the bits of brown earthenware and willow-patterned plates a small, broken pot: *Holloway's Universal Ointment for cuts, bruises, burns, chilblains, bad legs. 1/1, 2/9, 4/6, 11/-, 22/-, 33/- per pot.* I wonder how many bad legs the 33 shilling pot will cover! On the other side a Trade Mark: A doleful woman in a Grecian robe stands in front of a sideboard. Her right hand holds a cone from which a snake is feeding. The snake entwines a pillar topped with flames. Under the woman's other hand, a smaller woman holding a placard: NEVER DESPAIR.

Earth Time, Water and Sky

I poke around in the pile but the little pot keeps drawing me back. I hide it in a crack.
I'm halfway home when I realise the message from the old house.

> chuckles on
> the wind - the gods
> of rubbish dumps

The next day I go back to find the pot. It is sitting right on the top of the pile.

> I hold an oyster shell
> think of Hypatia - scraped flesh
> from bones by monks

Note: Hypatia, a learned woman of 5th century Alexandria, was hacked to death with oyster shells picked from a refuse heap.

---

meditating
in the dark
dawn birdsong

> Venetian steps
> my daughter flirts with
> passing boatmen

> old love letters
> smoulder
> in the grate

Spring Moon

After several years of illness in my mid fifties I feel very fit. I enjoy walking again, cycling, sawing logs At 60 I buy my Senior Railcard, go free into the Tate St Ives, start to iron my shirts. Clothes are the wrong shape. I break another tooth. The dentist counts the remainder; more than the stipulated number for National Health dentures. I read French books to test my memory; forget what I've come upstairs for. I wander round our field looking at the trees. Who will tend them when I'm gone? My mother's sewing box, the enduringness of *things!* I think of the gypsies who burn the possessions of the dead. Each day *another dinner nearer to death.*

spring moon
shadows loose skin on
my ageing hand

each time I pass
a mirror a glimpse
of my mother's face

dust motes
in a shaft of sunlight
the empty room

Water and Sky

Earth Time, Water and Sky

smooth over stones
the sound of water

beneath the old tree
the tide flows in
flows out

clifftop scant
of wild white roses
surf curls up the beach

swift pierces
skylark's song
the glittering sea

silence after rain
only the sound of water
seeping underground

surge and ebb of spring tide
curling up the sea wall - ghost
of my mother

lazy afternoon
sound of the surf
mist on the sea

Dwarfed by Space

Steep steps up from the beach to the Minack, open-air theatre on the cliff. Pausing to catch our breath we recall dramas played out with backdrop of moonlit sea and *The Magic Flute* in the rain. Granite coastline. Square jointed rock piles stand over little sandy bays, tropical turquoise sea. Beside the path St Levan's Well. The well water, known for treatment of eye problems and toothache, is still used for baptisms in St Levan's Church.

> where holy man
> blessed
> tadpoles swim

On Gwenapp Head, the Coastguard Station; a notice tells us: *Weather fine, visibility good, wind force 3 ENE. Path dry, take care at cliff edge.* My friend clutches my arm. On the path ahead a monstrous bird lifts up its beak, turns to look at us. Airborne it shrinks over open sea.

> bell buoy
> echoes
> raven's croak

The buoy marks The Runnel Stones, site of many shipwrecks. One of these, the *Khyber*, shattered here on the night of March 15 1905. Twenty three men from the wreck lie in a communal grave in the nearby graveyard. My companion slips on the gravelly path, rolls over several times - luckily not near the cliff edge. Turning inland we miss the path, stumble into a bog of white orchids. Fields of cows, peas, barley. A buzzard flies above, wingspan dwarfed by space of sky.

St Levan Church, squat building of granite blocks. Behind the tower wisps of cloud radiate in all directions. The grave of the drowned from the ship *Khyber*. Another grave is haunted by a ship's bell, those who hear it doomed to die within a year.

> over the fields
> we walk
> the coffin path

Earth Time, Water and Sky

Mother of All That Lives or Moves *

Another rainy morning, our small plot of land hidden in mist. I turn on the tap and watch the water flow into the kettle. I wonder about life in a hot country, about women in a far away place.

****

With my family I work a small plot of land. We grow enough to feed ourselves and a little over to sell in the market for our other needs. The climate is hot and dry but there is water nearby and we use it for our crops. We tend the land carefully and the crops grow well. The work is hard but the life is healthy and the family well fed.

dawn freshness
scent of dung fires
kingfisher's flash

The land does not belong to us. One day the landowner takes the land from all the villagers. He uses it to grow cash crops; our country is in debt and needs to export.

My husband leaves for the city. I find a small piece of barren land; there I scrape a meagre living to feed my four children and my husband's mother. Water no longer runs close by; the landowner has diverted it to irrigate his crops. He sprays the crops with chemicals and now I must walk many hours a day to find clean water. Every day my children's hunger, their gaunt grandmother. Sometimes I work for the landowner, spraying poisons on the land. The spray hurts my eyes and it's hard to breathe but my children can eat.

A foreign company builds a factory near to the water. My country allows this, they are in debt; though the factory will not serve to reduce the debt but only enrich foreigners. The earth is covered in concrete. The air is unbreathable. And the water! The water flowing out of the factory is foul. Now I must go even further to find water. I rise at 5.00 am. I set off in the dark with a pot on my head and one in each hand. I do not return until noon.

****

the kettle boils
rain still falls
the bitterness of cocoa.

*One of the names of the River Ganges

Moor Time

Earth squelches beneath my feet and the moor is empty of both sheep and humans. As I near my destination I see several parked cars. Dozemary Pool, on Bodmin Moor, is on the King Arthur trail. Going down the rough, walled track the lake sparkles ahead. I pass a group of people talking of Tintagel and sit on a stone near the water. A little boy comes to talk to me.

wind blows silver trails
across the lake. Small boy dreams
of Excalibur

This pool is identified with the legendary lake into which King Arthur's sword was thrown at his death. Here the hand of the Lady of the Lake caught the sword and brandished it three times before taking it beneath the water where it awaits rediscovery. The little boy talks of draining the lake to find the sword. He shows me his souvenir of Cornwall.

small child with new pen-
knife discovers the sponge
inside a reed

Alone after everyone leaves, I watch the light on the lake.

swallows skim
the surface catching glints
of sunshine

Returning to the car I'm surprised how much time has passed. When I arrive home I find that the clock in the car has jumped on an hour.

On Top of the World

Dawn. Sun touches the highest peaks as I set out to climb the crag above the town of Leh, Ladakh. Every day a monk offers early morning prayers in two small gompas* on this hill. The path has been washed away in recent rain and the scree slides beneath me. I thread my way up to the lowest monastery.

> buildings blend with rock
> strings of coloured flags flutter
> against the sky

Usually a few tourists come to view the gompas at opening time but today I am the only one among a crowd of Ladakhis coming up the path from the other side. I ask a man if it is a special occasion.
'No', he replies. 'Once every month we put up new prayer flags. On a day that is good,' he adds.

On the summit, in the ruins of a third gompa a fire is lit, fed with butter and herbs. Long poles are embedded in the edge of the precipice.

> young men hang in air
> with bundles of bright flags
> new links cross the valley

Chanting begins. I hang back, fearing to intrude but a smiling woman takes my hand, draws me into the circle. We have no words in common; I sit beside her in silence as sound flows round us with smell of butter and fragrant smoke. Every now and then my neighbour throws rice into the air, stops for a chat or points out something in the town below, then turns the pages of her book to join the chants again. The script is in Tibetan but the page numbers are familiar. She is reading from page 24. Sunshine moves over the plain. Below, the cramped town, a few fields, small patch on a desert landscape. Early morning chill; sun withdraws in a cloudy sky, the wind is sharp. The prayers reach page 43.

> voices
> rise in space
> surrounded by nameless snow peaks

*Monasteries

Earth Time, Water and Sky

The chanting ends, after 86 pages, with sudden joyful shouts. We all stand and
sampa is passed round.
Throw up', someone says to me.
I throw the flour into the air to general laughter as it falls on the head of a nearby
youth. He shakes it out of his hair.
Not yet. Watch me.'
Everyone begins to sing. We raise our fistfuls of flour three times. No longer a
stranger I am part of this hilltop communion as we cast our flour on the wind. It
rises in a fine cloud.

flour blows where we
can't go   towards mountains
which guard Tibet

February noon
dark against the grey
a buzzard soars

alone in the mist
sea
lapping my feet

on top of the dunes
only blue sky
and larksong

Mountain Reflections

The bus drives away leaving darkness. I stumble down the rough drive until, turning a corner, lights, greetings. After supper the retreat begins in silence. The days have a pattern: meditate, walk, listen, question, discuss.

> sound of the gong
> lingers - early
> morning yawns

By the second afternoon backs begin to ache. Behind the Buddha rain and sunlight cross the mountain, rainbows shimmer in the mist, the farmer tends his sheep. We settle into the stillness.

> in the silence
> intense irritation flips
> to affection

As the week moves on, assumptions are questioned. What do we know about time, space, ourselves and the world? Attitudes are shaken, common sense challenged. Feelings of outrage, of wanting to leave. We take comfort in food, walk down to the lake where rams, with ripe testicles, eye ewes across the fence. In the water mountain reflections shatter in ripples.

Something shifts in my solid worldview. Earnestness cracks into laughter.

The trains are disrupted by engineering works so I leave early, return up the drive in grey dawn

> clouds
> hide the mountain
> hum of morning chants